D1214149

All-American Fighting Forces

GO FOR BROKE REGIMENT

JULIA GARSTECKI

WORLD BOOK
BOLT

This World Book edition of *Go For Broke Regiment* is published by agreement between Black Rabbit Books and World Book, Inc.
© 2017 Black Rabbit Books,
2140 Howard Dr. West,
North Mankato, MN 56003 U.S.A.
World Book, Inc.,
180 North LaSalle St., Suite 900,
Chicago, IL 60601 U.S.A.

All rights reserved. No part of this book may be reproduced in any form without written permission from the publisher.

Design and Production by Michael Sellner
Photo Research by Rhonda Milbrett

Library of Congress Control Number: 2015954842

HC ISBN: 978-0-7166-9670-4   PB ISBN: 978-0-7166-9671-1

Printed in the United States at CG Book Printers,
North Mankato, Minnesota, 56003. PO #1794 4/16

Image Credits
Alamy: nsf, 27; Corbis: 10; Getty: Eliot Elisofon / Contributor, Cover; National Archives and Records Administration: Back Cover, 1, 3, 4–5, 6, 9 (ship), 12–13, 14–15, 16, 18–19, 20, 23, 24, 28–29, 32; Shutterstock: Gary Blakeley, 26; Joshya, 28–29; Kositlimsiri, 9 (Japan); Markus Reed, 31; Oceloti, 9 (bottom); Robert Biedermann/Shutterstock, 9 (Oahu); Seita, 15; Sovenko Artem, 21
Every effort has been made to contact copyright holders for material reproduced in this book. Any omissions will be rectified in subsequent printings if notice is given to the publisher.

Contents

4

CHAPTER 1

Fighting Bravely

The enemy surrounded more than 200 U.S. soldiers. Others tried to rescue them. They failed. Then came the men of the 442nd **Regiment**.

Creeping through fog, the men circled the enemy. Then they charged. For three days, the men battled. Finally, the enemy gave up. The soldiers were free. But almost half the men of the 442nd were dead.

Never Give Up

The men of the 442nd were soldiers in World War II. Their battle cry was "go for broke." This saying meant they would die before giving up. This saying became the group's nickname.

The soldiers fought for the United States. But they also fought to be treated fairly. The men of the 442nd were Japanese Americans. Many people in the United States disliked people from Japan. But the men still fought and died for their country.

CHAPTER 2

World War II

In 1939, Germany attacked Poland. That action started World War II. Japan and Italy joined Germany. The **Allies** fought against them.

In December 1941, Japan bombed a U.S. base in Hawaii. The attack destroyed military ships and planes. The United States **declared** war on Japan. U.S. soldiers joined the Allies.

Attack on Pearl Harbor

Japan

Tokyo

island of
Oahu,
Hawaii

Pearl
Harbor

Locked Up

The Japanese attack scared people.
Some worried Japanese Americans
were spies. The U.S. government
forced Japanese Americans into camps.
Barbed wire surrounded the camps.
Guards with guns watched the people
night and day.

Japanese American Internment Camps

- Amache, Colorado
- Gila River, Arizona
- Heart Mountain, Wyoming
- Jerome, Arkansas
- Manzanar, California
- Minidoka, Idaho
- Poston, Arizona
- Rohwer, Arkansas
- Topaz, Utah
- Tule Lake, California

Needing Help

By 1943, the United States needed more soldiers. The U.S. military asked men from the camps to fight. The Japanese Americans were locked up unfairly. But many men still **volunteered**.

The men became part of the 442nd. This group trained in Mississippi. They learned to watch for enemies and use weapons. On April 22, 1944, they left for war.

WORLD WAR II
BY THE NUMBERS

MORE THAN
13,000
SERVED IN
THE 442nd

3,713
SOLDIERS FROM
THE 442ND WERE
WOUNDED

291,557
U.S. SOLDIERS DIED
IN BATTLE

650 SOLDIERS FROM THE 442ND WERE KILLED

16,112,566 U.S. soldiers fought

The 442nd fought bravely in the battle in Italy. More than 1,000 men were killed, wounded, or went missing.

CHAPTER 3

The in Battle

Japanese American soldiers fought bravely throughout **Europe**. A battle in Italy dragged on for months. Finally, in April 1945, the 442nd climbed a steep mountain. The climb was dangerous, and some men fell. But even in death, they did not scream.

Fighting On

The men of the 442nd surprised the enemy. German soldiers attacked back. Many men were hit with bullets or grenades. But the soldiers of the 442nd fought on. They killed 25 enemies.

PARTS OF THE 442nd COMBAT TEAM

100th Infantry Battalion

2nd Battalion

3rd Battalion

442nd Infantry Battalion

522nd Field Artillery Battalion

232nd Combat Engineers

Regimental Headquarters Company

jeep cap

shelter

cartridge
belt

boots ▶

helmets

radio

CHAPTER 4

Coming **Home**

World War II ended in 1945. The soldiers returned home. The men of the 442nd were heroes. They received more than 18,000 awards. The 442nd is one of the most **decorated** units in military history.

Awards for the 442nd

Award	Count
Purple Heart	
Bronze Star	
Silver Star	588
Distinguished Service Cross	52
Presidential Unit Citation	8
Medal of Honor	21

0

9,486

4,000

2,000 4,000 6,000 8,000 10,000

Closing Camps

After the war, Japanese Americans were let out of the camps. They had been away from their homes for nearly four years. Many had nothing to go home to. Soldiers and their families had to start new lives.

Japanese Americans during WWII

120,000 people held in camps

Two-thirds of the people had never been to Japan.

Never Give Up

The 442nd is still active today. It's still known for soldiers who never give up.

The Japanese American soldiers were brave. Their country didn't always love them. But they loved their country.

The men of the 442nd earned nearly 9,500 Purple Hearts. This award is given to soldiers who are wounded or killed.

DECEMBER 1941

The United States enters World War II.

FEBRUARY 1943

442nd Regiment is created.

1942

1943

1944

MARCH 1943

Japanese Americans are asked to join the military.

APRIL 1944
442nd goes to Europe.

1947
442nd becomes part of the Army Reserve.

1945   1946   1947

September 1945
World War II ends.

GLOSSARY

Allies (al-EYZ)—the United States, Great Britain, Soviet Union, France, and other countries that fought against Germany, Italy, and Japan during World War II

battalion (buh-TAL-yun)—a large organized group of soldiers

declare (de-KLAYR)—to say or state something in an official way

decorate (DEH-ko-rayt)—to give a medal or award to someone

Europe (YUR-up)—the sixth largest continent

regiment (REH-juh-muhnt)—a military unit made of several battalions

volunteer (vol-un-TEER)—to give up time to help someone or something

BOOKS

Adams, Simon. *World War II.* Eyewitness Books. New York: DK Publishing, 2014.

Collier, Peter. *Choosing Courage: True Stories of Heroism from Soldiers and Civilians.* New York: Artisan Books, 2015.

Sandler, Martin W. *Imprisoned: The Betrayal of Japanese Americans During World War II.* New York: Walker Books for Young Readers, 2013.

WEBSITES

442nd Regimental Combat Team
www.the442.org/home.html

The Famous 442nd: Japanese-Americans Fought Fiercely for America
www.socialstudiesforkids.com/articles/ushistory/442nd.htm

Fighting for Democracy
www.pbs.org/thewar/at_war_democracy_japanese_american.htm

Japanese-American Internment
www.ushistory.org/us/51e.asp

INDEX

AUG _ _ 2017

FREDERICK COUNTY PUBLIC LIBRARIES